aves
Reviv
ect the Unexpec

WAVES OF REVIVAL

WAVES OF REVIVAL

Second Edition

Expect the Unexpected

BILL VINCENT

Waves of Revival
Copyright © 2016 by Bill Vincent. All rights reserved.

No part of this publication may be reproduced, stored in a retrieval system or transmitted in any way by any means, electronic, mechanical, photocopy, recording or otherwise without the prior permission of the author except as provided by USA copyright law.

Published By
Revival Waves of Glory Books & Publishing
PO Box 596
Litchfield, IL 62056
http://www.revivalwavesofgloryministries.com

Revival Waves of Glory Books & Publishing is committed to excellence in the publishing industry.

Published in the United States of America

Paperback: 978-1-62676-925-0

TABLE OF CONTENTS

INTRODUCTION 5
THE SPIRIT OF REVIVAL 7
A FORETASTE OF THE PAST 20
GREAT HEALING REVIVAL 34
THE HEALING MANTLE 56
MAINTAIN REVIVAL 61
SIGNS AND WONDERS OF TODAY 66
REVIVAL OF THE BOOK OF ACTS 74
WILLIAM BRANHAM 79
THE HEALING MOVEMENT 88
ABOUT THE AUTHOR 93

RECOMMENDED PRODUCTS 95

INTRODUCTION

I have personally experienced revivals breaking out several times and we are sure to see many more to come. Revival seems to be the main topic on people's lips. We have a lot to learn from all those in history of past revivals. God has been getting a remnant of people ready for the next coming waves of revival. God all over the world is putting together a people that will truly be sold out for revival. There are many whom say the right words and say they are sold out, but when things heat up where are they. God is speaking of a coming healing revival that is unlike this world has seen. Are you ready? It is time to prepare your heart for waves of revival. This is where you never know what to expect next.

THE SPIRIT OF REVIVAL

Revival is more than just something put on a sign outside of your local Church. Revival comes from the Spirit of God. The Spirit of Revival honors those who press in and move the heart of God. I will share how my ravenous hunger for Jesus Christ drove me in hot pursuit of God's presence, and then the amazing way that God responded. First I'll explain why it's vital to remember God's hand of intervention in your life and how remembering activates several important keys, keys that will drive you further and deeper into God's purposes. At the end I'll discuss, from personal experience, the secret I learned about cultivating and maintaining intimacy with God. You will also discover how your desperation for fellowship with God will propel you into the spirit of revival.

Holy Ghost come today! Come in power, that there would be an increase, Holy Spirit, an increase of Your anointing. That we would feel You like a mighty wind rushing, blowing, falling in a new way, a fresh way. I pray for a fresh fire, God. I pray for that fire and that revival spirit to come! Let the revival spirit that can stir a whole generation grip our hearts so that we become burning, shining lamps of revival!

God I pray that you raise up "John the Baptists," that you raise up the fiery witnesses that you raise up the fiery preachers today! I'm asking that you raise up the apostolic

Elijah ministry that you raise up the power encounters; that you raise up the radical worshippers and a fierce, abandoned generation that's love sick and all they want is Jesus.

God make them to be a witness of the truth, bold and strong. It's an encounter with your Spirit; it's the power of God, and it's the anointing that's going to do it today Lord! Let the fire fall. Let the Spirit of revival come! Thank you Lord. Amen! O that God would stir our hearts with passion; that we would encounter Him with such abandon that we could all say: "God, I'm as hungry for you today as I was at any other time in my life!" Yes! I want to be challenged and provoked too. I'm preaching to myself today as I write this Chapter today!

Passion (for God) climbs to new heights when you're absolutely desperate for Him.

Psalms 42:1, 2 **To the chief Musician, Maschil, for the sons of Korah.** As the hart panteth after the water brooks, so panteth my soul after thee, O God. My soul thirsteth for God, for the living God: when shall I come and appear before God?

Panting! Thirsting! But thirsting for what? The answer is here "When shall I come and appear before God?" Literally what he is saying is, "When will I have a visitation of God appearing to me?" It's not about us appearing before people. It's about us appearing before God.

The psalmist goes on to say:
Psalms 42:6, 7 O my God, my soul is cast down within me: therefore will I remember thee from the land of Jordan, and of the Hermonites, from the hill Mizar. Deep calleth unto deep

at the noise of thy waterspouts: all thy waves and thy billows are gone over me.

All your waves and billows have gone over me. It's not just one wave. It's wave after wave of God's glory and anointing! There is a momentum here.

Rev 2:4, 5 Nevertheless I have *somewhat* against thee, because thou hast left thy first love. Remember therefore from whence thou art fallen, and repent, and do the first works; or else I will come unto thee quickly, and will remove thy candlestick out of his place, except thou repent.

Wow. "You have left your first love." We can all think of those days when we were hungrier and more radical for God, devouring our Bible every day. Maybe for you it was in those first few months that you were a Christian. But now, because of some hard trials, valleys, and disappointments, you realize that you're still walking with God, still reading the Bible and going to church, but there's something missing. It's like there's only a hint of the smell of what was once there. For some of you, it's such a faint memory.

Jesus Christ is challenging us, so let's be honest. We need to fall in love with Jesus again revisit our first love. And I know we're faced with our own carnality and by how unspiritual we are sometimes. In my own life, as spiritual as I've been at times I could be hungrier and more on fire. So then, what is the key to awakening our first love? The answer is found in the scripture we just read "remember therefore from where you have fallen."

There's something about when we begin to remember and we begin to allow the Holy Spirit to move in the imagination, taking us back to the greatest times of, God's power coming in our lives. It's important to remember those times when we were really hungry. The problem is, sometimes we just accept being lukewarm as normal. But Jesus said to "remember therefore from where you have fallen" and then He goes on to say, "repent and do the first works."

When God speaks to me about the fire, the hunger, the anointing, the glory, and revival, He says to remember.

So now, when God says to repent and do the first works, I always remember how I would go after His presence. I always remember how I'd wait for another wave. I always remember how I learned to move in the anointing. I always remember how I'd say, "Come Holy Spirit." I always remember how I'd wait and how I would soak. I always remember the fire and the ravenous hunger and the passion. Because when I remember, it stirs up my passion and hunger for God! It brings me back to my first love, Jesus!

I remember one of the first times that God appeared to me. I was so hungry. I moved in the gifts of the Spirit, I was really excited about that, and I just wanted to prophesy over anything that moved. I told the Lord, "You know what I really want You and Your presence." Simultaneously there was something in my heart that was challenged and I heard the Lord say, "Hey, Bill. I know you're tired, but can you spend another hour in prayer? Will you love Me when the meeting is over?" And so I thought: You know what, Lord. I want to go home and just love on You because that's the only reason this (ministry) all happens. I love Him more than the gift (the anointing).

You see, even though I had the joy of giving a prophetic word, I just wanted to get to my place and worship the Lord. (It's easy to pray before a meeting because you want to be anointed but it's your attitude when the meeting is over that reveals your true character. So much of what I do is because I have a meeting. My challenge is to do what I do because I love Jesus.) So when I got to my place, I thought: God I am going to honor You and I am waiting on You. As I was lying in my bed, I was thinking, God, You are beautiful, You are awesome. I love you! Forget all about the gifts and the power, I'm just back here at four in the morning now and I'm loving You.

After a while; Hallelujah, the presence of God is all around me and somebody has just stepped into my room! It was so real.

Today, by remembering this encounter with Jesus, my passion for Him is ignited once again! You see, that's the cry here in Psalms 42 I am panting, my soul is longing, I'm thirsting for God, for the living God and here is what I'm hungry for: When shall I come and appear before God? When will God appear to me? I need an encounter. I need a visitation. I need an experience.

Psalms 42:3, 4 My tears have been my meat day and night, while they continually say unto me, Where *is* thy God? When I remember these *things,* I pour out my soul in me: for I had gone with the multitude, I went with them to the house of

God, with the voice of joy and praise, with a multitude that kept holyday.

There's a whole world out there, a mocking world, that's saying today, "Where is your God?" Maybe it comes through some of your mocking friends, family, relationships, or circumstances "Where is your God?"

Maybe it isn't even people, family, or those you're in relationship with that are saying it, but your own soul is saying, "Yeah, where is God? There are times when Christians get so hopeless and disappointed; so discouraged. I know this is happening among young people and they are saying, "Where is the Lord God of Elijah? Where is the God that we read about in the Bible? Where is the power, where is the reality, where is the presence? I'm in the valley, man. I'm battling."

If there is lukewarmness, you have to take responsibility for it. It's not always the church's fault. You've got to stir yourself up to take hold of God and go to the well yourself and go to the river of God yourself. You need to say, "I don't just want to go to where the blessing is, I want to be the blessing. I don't just want to go to the revival, I want to carry the revival. I want to be what starts the revival!

Psalms 42:5 Why art thou cast down, O my soul? and *why* art thou disquieted in me? hope thou in God: for I shall yet praise him *for* the help of his countenance.

Here is a big key that will help you overcome all that junk "Hope in God for I shall yet praise Him for the help of His countenance." In other words be determined to walk into that field of praise, as hard as it is. Just open up your mouth and praise Him; He is worthy, regardless of how you feel. You've got to be at a place where you stop and say, "Soul, what are you doing, and why are you so complacent? I've got to remember from where I have fallen.

I've got to get back that love and that passion and that fire; I've got to get it back! I've got to get rocked again! I've got to repent and do the first works! Something's wrong here. I'm not going to stay here anymore murmuring and going around this mountain. I am going to do something about it!"

Psalms 42:6, 7 O my God, my soul is cast down within me: therefore will I remember thee from the land of Jordan, and of the Hermonites, from the hill Mizar. Deep calleth unto deep at the noise of thy waterspouts: all thy waves and thy billows are gone over me.

Waves! We're waiting for another wave. It's worth repeating it's not just one wave. It's wave after wave of God's glory and anointing! I want you to think about that.

As you prepare your heart for the rest of this Chapter, start remembering what God has done for you. Ask the Holy Spirit if there are any areas where you need to repent and then deal with those issues. For some, you're coming to realize that you've left your first love. Don't get into condemnation.

Revelations 2:5 Remember therefore from whence thou art fallen, and repent, and do the first works; or else I will come unto thee quickly, and will remove thy candlestick out of his place, except thou repent.

Also, just to wet your appetite, let me tell you that next I'm going to share a secret that has the potential to transform your ability to maintain intimacy with the Lord so that you can abide in the momentum of His glory and anointing.

God wants us to be carriers of His glory and anointing moment by moment, hour by hour, and day by day! There is a momentum, like riding a wave; a momentum that comes in prayer, in the glory and in the anointing, God wants us to abide in all the time.

Something changed the first time I said, "Holy Spirit I want to know you!" It was like my prayer life went from ten to one hundred! Everything speeds up to the next level just because I invited the Holy Spirit to come.

Yes, I was already baptized and speaking in tongues, but I knew there was more.

I remembered God's word,

Matthew 7:7 Ask, and it shall be given you; seek, and ye shall find; knock, and it shall be opened unto you:

Psalms 91:15 He shall call upon me, and I will answer him: I *will be* with him in trouble; I will deliver him, and honour him.

But in my desperation and hunger, the Lord did visit me! I would have these incredible times in the glory. I mean I couldn't even get off the floor sometimes for hours and hours. It would feel like electricity was going through my body. But, then all of a sudden, the visitation would stop and I would wonder why the Spirit had left me.

Well, I learned something. God never leaves, we do.

Matthew 28:20 Teaching them to observe all things whatsoever I have commanded you: and, lo, I am with you alway, *even* unto the end of the world. Amen.

Have you ever been in the presence of God and it's so great you wonder why you would ever leave? Or when you are in the anointing you wonder why you ever left the last time. And then, you realize that you didn't pray all week, or you left last time because your family needed you or a friend called. You know what I mean.

Something else I came to realize is that the biggest thing about connecting with the presence of God is learning to still the mind learning to focus. Worship helps us focus. Have you ever felt a wave come in your own prayer life maybe you were praying in tongues or you were worshipping, you have some music playing, and you are praying in the very presence of God when all of a sudden His presence just lifts. The minute we break that flow and that momentum, the wave is gone. He was there and then He disappeared.

I've noticed that some of the time God's presence lifts for no apparent reason. Here I am pressing in, God's presence comes, and then all of a sudden, it's gone. It's like no more anointing. No more presence of God. No more feeling of the glory. So I just want to move on and do something else.

Yet, God never let me move on to do my own thing. Instead, He began to teach me how to stay in the flow of His Spirit.

One day I was pressing in maybe an hour soaking in God's presence, and then it just lifted. So I got up and thought: You know what God, I want more. I'm going to press in again as if I didn't even pray that last hour. I am going to pretend that hour didn't even happen. So I started praying as if I was just starting from the very beginning put on the CD and started worshipping. Even though I'd already prayed an hour I began pressing in as if I'd not even prayed. Then God came! I stayed on the floor for an hour but then it was like God was gone again and so I thought: Where is God going?

My impression was that He wasn't leaving completely but the intensity of that fire was gone. And then a revelation came to me. I got up and thought: How hungry am I? My challenge was this: Am I going to wait and press in for another wave and go deeper, or stop? I began to realize that God was moving the boundary. By that I mean, it was like He was saying: "Come on son. Hide, and go seek. Come on son. Come on a little bit deeper." Well, that was it! I started chasing God!

I'll never forget that first time when hours went by pressing in, God would leave, I'd give chase, and God would come and catch me. God would leave, I'd chase Him again. He would come and catch me, and then He would leave and I'd chase Him again! We went back and forth for hours until I got so deep I was thinking: I'm really out here in the heavens. I'd don't know if I'm ever going to get back to earth!

When God's manifest presence comes and then His presence decreases, what should we do? We wait for another wave. We press in for another wave and we stay hungry. That's the secret that God taught me and that is the challenge for me and for you.

I did that for months, hours a day. God gave me such determination, and this brought results. You see, there is this momentum that comes in prayer that enables us to ride the waves of God's glory and anointing. There is a momentum that God wants each of us to abide in all the time.

I realized on the one hand that if I kept pursuing God everyday an incredible breakthrough would happen, but on the other hand, if I stopped (praying) for two or three days, it was hard to get back in the flow. Five days might go by with no real prayer, and I'd still be thinking that I was going to go back into the glory like I had the previous week. Not! I'd go back to prayer and it was the hardest thing to do. It was like starting all over again. As a result, I took it seriously to continually build up "this place" in prayer and to keep pressing in for the anointing. For example, I would start feeling the presence of God and then the next day God's presence would come in less time, perhaps only twenty minutes, and then the following day I'd experience God's presence after only about a minute. Then the next day it was like no effort there He is! The same for the next day He was waiting for me!

Cultivating and maintaining intimacy with God goes hand in hand with pursuing Him constantly. In fact, that's the way we learn how to wait for the next wave and how we learn to press in deeper and ride the momentum of God's glory and anointing. If you get hungry enough to wait and you begin to pray and if the Spirit of God comes, that momentum will carry you through the night and the next day and it will carry you into the next week and the next month! As a matter of fact, when you get a grace and a momentum and a spark and a fire, you've got to ride the wave!

You don't have to stay in your prayer closet in order to ride God's waves. You see, there is a wave in the anointing and when you hit the wave and experience the momentum, you'll start moving in the anointing. For some, you'll be getting out on the streets evangelizing. For others, you'll start prophesying and your gift will get sharper and sharper. You'll be hitting this "groove," but you need to stay hungry for God to stay in the groove!

Exodus 24:15-18 And Moses went up into the mount, and a cloud covered the mount. And the glory of the LORD abode upon mount Sinai, and the cloud covered it six days: and the seventh day he called unto Moses out of the midst of the cloud. And the sight of the glory of the LORD *was* like devouring fire on the top of the mount in the eyes of the children of Israel. And Moses went into the midst of the cloud, and gat him up into the mount: and Moses was in the mount forty days and forty nights.

Exodus 33:9 And it came to pass, as Moses entered into the tabernacle, the cloudy pillar descended, and stood *at* the door of the tabernacle, and *the LORD* talked with Moses.

That is God's challenge to all of us today! There is a contagious holy provoking from God "How hungry are you?" This holy confrontation drives me to be concerned that you have an encounter with God and that your heart cries: "God, I want to know You!"

If I could give you anything it would be an impartation of holy hunger, desperation, anointing, and Holy Spirit presence. These four manifestations combined with the cry, "God I want to know You," mark what it takes to release the spirit of revival. In fact, I believe there is that kind of revival spirit here today! That's what this generation needs to catch! You see, I got really hungry, and so can you! I said, "Holy Spirit I don't know You in fellowship. But remember, before we can actually ride those waves, we need to return to our first love, Jesus Christ. That's why I shared some of my testimony in this Chapter, because I thought if this generation is really going to catch any of what God wants to release, I need to share what I did in the beginning. How we paid the price and how important it is to rekindle our first love for Jesus. Part of that is my own journey right now.

It's time to have an encounter with God. Are you ready to stir yourself up and remember the grace from which you've fallen, and repent and go back to those first works? How about you? Are you challenged in your prayerlessness and the routine of what Christianity has become and you're ready to say: "Soul, why have you become cast down?"

Let's invite the Holy Spirit to come. I just love being in His presence and seeing Him show up and mess people up. We get so polished sometimes, in such a routine. What if God came down and just wrecked our whole paradigm and shook us to the core? "Come, Holy Spirit, I invite you. Come into my life, touch everything. Shake me, visit me, and change me." Just begin to pray now.

A FORETASTE OF THE PAST

We can have great Revival in the present when we truly see a taste of the past. One of the first things I did when Revival broke out in Litchfield, IL was study history. I wanted to learn from past revivals and ministries who walked in the miraculous.

Deuteronomy 32:7 Remember the days of old, consider the years of many generations: ask thy father, and he will shew thee; thy elders, and they will tell thee.

This warning, given to Israel through Moses, required the children of Israel to examine their past and gain understanding about the Lord's ways. This same thing has even greater value today as we challenge ourselves to understand our Christian heritage and learn about God's sovereignty and His dealings with man. While we do not want to live in the past, we can examine and extract from the past, nuggets of wisdom concerning God's ways with His church. Since the days of the Reformation, the Lord has brought a progressive revelation of Himself to the church. This revelation has been line upon line and precept upon precept continually unfolding fresh revelation of Himself and His Word.

This process is for the purpose of restoring the church to her former apostolic authority as realized in the first century church. As we consider the prior generations, we can relish the revelation given to them and also learn from their mistakes in order to avoid those same mistakes in our generation.

Apostolic ministry can be defined as Jesus Christ manifested and abiding in His church doing the same works through His church that He did while living on the earth in human form. True apostolic ministry is a fulfillment of John 14:12, with the Holy Spirit performing the same works through the church that He did through the life and ministry of the Lord Jesus Christ.

John 14:12 Verily, verily, I say unto you, He that believeth on me, the works that I do shall he do also; and greater *works* than these shall he do; because I go unto my Father.

There is a ministry of perfection coming to the church that will prepare her for the return of the Bridegroom. However, before we can begin to move toward this ministry, we must first "return back to our future" and realize the complete restoration of biblical apostolic ministry. This ministry will call out and separate the church from the world so that she can be prepared in perfection for the Bridegroom.

Joel 2:25 And I will restore to you the years that the locust hath eaten, the cankerworm, and the caterpiller, and the palmerworm, my great army which I sent among you.

There are four stages of a maturing locust used to prophetically symbolize the way that the spirit of the antichrist would attack the church. The early apostolic church is like a tree that the Lord planted and nurtured to full fruit bearing maturity. The spirit of the antichrist is compared to a locust which devours first the fruit, then the leaves, the bark and finally gnawing into the very heart of the tree in order to destroy it.

In church history, this final stage culminated in the era known as the Dark Ages. The Lord's promise to restore the apostolic church began through the ministry of Martin Luther and has now matured to a level so that this generation can expect the complete restoration of biblical apostolic ministry. This is our quest: to return back to the future. When our Lord was on the earth, He chose the 12 apostles to groom and prepare for the birth of His apostolic church. For three and one half years, He planted the seed of the Word of God within their hearts. When the day of Pentecost had fully come, the Holy Spirit descended upon them and watered the seed within their hearts, producing the life of Christ and the apostolic church. This same process must be realized in this church age as well.

Tokens of Apostolic Ministry throughout church history, there have been examples of true apostolic ministry raised up by the Lord within the church. These individuals attained a mature stature qualifying them as a dwelling place for the Spirit of God through whom the Lord was able to function and do His works. They were men and women so thoroughly filled with the Holy Spirit that they exercised the Lord's dominion over demons, disease and death. These saints were true expressions of the life of Christ with His divine nature radiating through them men and women who were crucified with Christ and lived by the faith of the Son of God. Tremendous lessons can be learned by examining the lives of these spiritual champions in order to determine the secrets of their success with God.

One example of true apostolic ministry can be found in the life of John Graham Lake. An Apostle of Faith By every biblical definition, the life of John G. Lake demonstrated the nature and characteristics of true apostolic ministry. John G. Lake was a man who experienced apostolic ministry according to first century standards and changed the world everywhere he went. He was a vessel yielded to God as a habitation for His manifest presence. Through him, the Holy Spirit was able to heal the sick, cast out demons, save the lost, and manifest the very nature and character of Christ, displaying that Jesus Christ is the same yesterday, today and forever.

Hebrews 13:8 Jesus Christ the same yesterday, and to day, and for ever.

The Great Commission was a reality, not a theory, in Lake's ministry. Careful examination of his life will help the church to prepare for the coming visitation and restoration of the apostolic ministry. Having the Lord's Potential, John 12:24 Verily, verily, I say unto you, Except a corn of wheat fall into the ground and die, it abideth alone: but if it die, it bringeth forth much fruit.

When the time came for the Lord to be glorified through the sacrificial offering of His life, He compared His life with a grain of wheat. When a grain of wheat dies, it is for the purpose of bringing forth multiplied grains of wheat like the original grain. The Bible teaches that when the Lord returns, we will be like Him. The Holy Spirit residing in us will reveal the same attributes through us that He did in the Lord Jesus Christ.

This belief formed the cornerstone for John G. Lake's life and ministry. Lake believed that the Lord would not have commissioned us to do the works that He did without adequately equipping us to do those works. Lake commented, "We need to set our sights high and refuse the traditions of men who say that it is impossible to do as Jesus instructed us." True apostolic ministry is simply the extension of the ministry begun by the Lord, our ultimate example. The power of redemption is so great that sinners saved by grace and filled with the Holy Spirit are given the opportunity of carrying on the very ministry of Christ, doing the works that He did. John G. Lake is a token of this reality given to the twentieth century. Our sights should be set equally high. His Definition of the Apostolic Church during the years preceding and following the turn of the twentieth century, John Lake made a notable and revealing observation. There had been a tremendous outpouring of the Holy Spirit with great manifestations of power, signs and wonders. A generation of Christians was given an extraordinary opportunity of witnessing the return of genuine apostolic ministry. Lake discerned that his generation missed the mark by not realizing the true definition of apostolic ministry. Some attempted to build an apostolic church around the doctrine and manifestation of healing power. Others attempted to establish the apostolic church around the restoration of the gifts and speaking in tongues, while some attempted to create and establish the apostolic order around the doctrine of holiness. All of these qualities are attributes of the Holy Spirit and essential to the church, yet not one singularly sustains apostolic ministry. Lake observed that the people were absorbed in the phenomena of God and not in the person of God. According to Lake, the truest definition of the apostolic church could be expressed in the awesome and reverential experience known as the baptism of the Holy Spirit. He believed that the church did not regard the baptism of the Holy Spirit with the reverence due an experience so sacred and so terribly costly.

In order to secure this gift for His church, the Lord Jesus lived in the world, bled on the cross, entered into the darkness of death, hell and the grave, wrestle with and strangled the powers of darkness, came forth in resurrection life and ascended to heaven.

Lake believed apostolic ministry was defined and realized through individuals becoming the habitation of God. The Holy Spirit literally manifested Himself in the spirit, soul and body of the believers, taking total possession of His church and bestowing on us His qualities and attributes. This process was not merely a reformation it was a renewal. Men and women were renewed by the Spirit of God, indwelt by the Holy Spirit and becoming one Spirit with Him. The baptism of the Holy Spirit was not merely a gift of power, but of God Himself. Out of necessity, Lake became acquainted with the healing power of God.

During the later years of the nineteenth century, he was miraculously healed of a terminal illness, along with his wife, his sister and his brother. This introduction to God's miraculous power caused Lake to begin a quest to not only know the healing of God, but to know the God of healing.

His desire was fulfilled, he describes, when he became the habitation of God in a powerful baptism of the Holy Spirit.

His Baptism Experience at the age of 16, John G. Lake came to know the saving power of Christ. His salvation experience was very real as displayed by his changed life. Many around him observed this change and said, "You are baptized in the Holy Ghost." While friends around him were saying that he had been filled with the Holy Spirit, Lake experienced an almost unbearable hunger in his heart for more of God. He began to pursue God and came to know the sanctifying power of the Holy Spirit through the ministry of a layman named Melvin Pratt. This precious brother introduced Lake to the washing of water by the Word, and this process increased the richness and anointing of Lake's life.

Those around him acknowledged that surely he had received the baptism of the Holy Spirit. Yet, Lake hungered for more. Several years later, Lake was introduced to the healing power of God through Alexander Dowie. After moving to Zion, Illinois to associate more closely with Dowie, Lake received a tremendous impartation of the healing power of God from the Holy Spirit. Many miracles and manifestations of the Spirit followed.

Those around Lake again tried to convince him that he had received the baptism of the Holy Spirit. By the turn of the century, John G. Lake had undergone a powerful salvation experience, an even more powerful sanctification experience, and an impartation of the gift of healing.

At each point in time, those around Lake tried to convince him that he had received the baptism of the Holy Spirit, yet his heart burned for more of God than ever before. Searching for that which would satisfy the longing of his heart, he began to fast, pray and wait upon the Lord for nine months. At the end of this period of prayer and fasting, Lake had an awesome experience with the Lord. He knew then that he had been immersed in the Holy Spirit and had finally become a dwelling place of God. His heart and soul were now satisfied that the Holy Spirit was residing in him, speaking through him, and saturating every fiber of his being. Finally his heart was content that he had received the baptism of the Holy Spirit which would produce the nature and character of Christ within him.

Lake believed, as the Scriptures taught, that this indwelling experience now equipped him to carry on the ministry of Christ as did the early apostles. In a study, Lake revealed the important significance of our complete redemption on all three levels of human life spirit, soul (mind) and body.

1 Thessalonians 5:23 And the very God of peace sanctify you wholly; and *I pray God* your whole spirit and soul and body be preserved blameless unto the coming of our Lord Jesus Christ.

Lake taught that it was the tendency of the average Christian to stop at the redemption of their spirit. He believed that it was equally as important for the believer to allow the Holy Spirit to sanctify the soul and the body in order for the individual to become the habitation of God. The sanctification of the soul literally involves the impartation of the mind of Christ.

John Wesley defined sanctification as "possessing the mind of Christ and all the mind of Christ." This level of consecration is essential for the believer's thoughts to be perfectly in tune with the Lord's thoughts and the Christian ways consistent with His ways. Complete sanctification of soul and mind also involves the renewal of the emotions. Many believers are trapped in the tyranny of grief over the past, not realizing that they are a new creation and that all things have become new

2 Corinthians 5:17 Therefore if any man *be* in Christ, *he is* a new creature: old things are passed away; behold, all things are become new.

Grief ultimately leads to bitterness, and bitterness will defile many.

Hebrews 12:15 Looking diligently lest any man fail of the grace of God; lest any root of bitterness springing up trouble *you,* and thereby many be defiled;

Consequently, it is essential that the Holy Spirit be allowed to thoroughly consecrate and sanctify the mind, and the emotions in order for Christians to become the tabernacle of the Holy Spirit. This Sermon Lake spoke also involves the separation of the believer from all that would defile, recognizing that the body is the temple of the Holy Spirit and should be consecrated accordingly.

Romans 8:11 But if the Spirit of him that raised up Jesus from the dead dwell in you, he that raised up Christ from the dead shall also quicken your mortal bodies by his Spirit that dwelleth in you.

This imparted life granted through the indwelling presence of the Holy Spirit will provide divine health and freedom from the lusts that are a result of man's fallen condition. Lake taught that the genuine Christian is a separated person separated forever to God in all the departments of life: body, soul and spirit are forever committed to God. This absolute consecration to God, or "triune salvation," is the real secret to the successful Christian life and essential to becoming the habitation of God. According to John G. Lake, this complete consecration to God makes the Christian a "Christ-man" and reveals the secret of life and communion with God received into the entire being through the Holy Spirit.

Hebrews 12:14 Follow peace with all *men,* and holiness, without which no man shall see the Lord:

Without holiness, the complete purposes of the church cannot be fulfilled. A Holy God can only dwell in a holy vessel. Lake said, "Think not that thou shalt attain the highest in God until within thine own soul a heavenly longing to be like Him who gave His life for us possesses our own heart." A holy and sanctified condition can only be realized when the fleshly nature is revealed. Once the weaknesses of the human soul are revealed, Christians then can call upon the grace of God to separate from them all that is ungodly, thereby purging the spirit, soul and body from every worldly tendency. As Lake once put it, "There arises in the heart the desire and prayer for the Spirit of God to eject, crucify and destroy every tendency of the opposition of the Holy Spirit." The hearts of men and women must be purged by the fire of the Holy Spirit and washed from every stain by the cleansing blood of Christ. Those who desire to be partakers of the nature of Christ must always feel the purging power of Christ within. Once the Holy Spirit takes up residence, there is a release of power through the indwelling Spirit to lift the believer above the lusts and desires of this world in order to live a holy and consecrated life. This desire for the purity of God's nature reveals a vital ingredient in the life and Ministry of John G. Lake.

As he stated in 1916, "Holiness is the character of God. The very substance of His being and the essence of His nature is purity." The purpose of God in the salvation of mankind is to produce in man a kindred holiness, a radiant purity like that of God Himself. Clothed in a Spirit of Humility Another important attribute in Lake's ministry was his commitment to living in a spirit of humility.

1 Peter 5:5 Likewise, ye younger, submit yourselves unto the elder. Yea, all *of you* be subject one to another, and be clothed with humility: for God resisteth the proud, and giveth grace to the humble.

If the church is to "return back to the future" to her true apostolic heritage, Christians must adhere to the qualities demonstrated by the apostolic fathers. Acts 20:19 Serving the Lord with all humility of mind, and with many tears, and temptations, which befell me by the lying in wait of the Jews:

That commitment to humility by the first century apostle burned equally as bright in the heart of John G. Lake, a twentieth century apostle. Lake desired to follow the example set by Moses and sought to be the meekest man in the land. By virtue of this commitment to humility, he was able to say, "the Spirit of God ran through my person like a river of heavenly fluid. Cancers withered under my touch, cripples of every type were instantly restored and works of creation in the bodies of men took place as a result of humbling myself under the mighty hand of God."

Like Moses, he desired to not only see the acts of an awesome God, but also to understand His ways. As a result, he discovered that the Lord's way was through servanthood and a spirit of humility clothing the believer.

It is only through amazing grace that the nature and works of Christ can be exhibited through believers. God gives His grace to the humble. Humility is truly a key ingredient to the restoration of true apostolic ministry and the return of the Shekinah glory to the church. The empowering presence as with the first century apostles, John G. Lake did not attempt full time ministry until he was endued with power from on high. Even though the early apostles had received an anointing from the Lord for casting out evil spirits and healing the sick, they did not become the dwelling place of God until the day of Pentecost. It is one thing to receive anointing or gifts from the Lord; it is altogether another to become the literal dwelling place of the manifest presence of God. Lake knew the reality of the empowering presence of God abiding within him.

He was anointed and equipped not only for ministering healing and salvation to a lost world, but also for expressing the radiant presence of a Holy God, or, as he explained it for, "becoming a Christ-man having all the potentials through the Holy Spirit that resided in Christ Himself." Lake spent a season of prayer and fasting specifically seeking a special anointing for casting out demons. The Lord graciously responded to the request of His servant by imparting a powerful anointing and the boldness necessary for dealing with evil spirits. As a result, people came from all over the world to be delivered and set free from demonic opposition. Tremendous testimonies are on record as evidence of this ministry. This empowering presence also carried Lake to a new level of understanding Scripture. Powerful and revelatory sermons emerged from this apostle of faith as he allowed the Holy Spirit to unfold the mysteries of the kingdom. He had the capacity to inspire faith in the hearts of those who heard him.

A man without compromise when it involved the Spirit's revelation of the Word, Lake utterly refused to compromise the true revelation of the Word for a false unity which he believed resulted in spiritual weakness. He believed that principle is better than unity, and the ultimate end of right principles would be true unity of the faith as described in,

Ephesians 4:13 Till we all come in the unity of the faith, and of the knowledge of the Son of God, unto a perfect man, unto the measure of the stature of the fulness of Christ:

Lake believed the secret to Christianity was not in doing but in being. It is in possessing the divine nature of Christ and His empowering presence that we become the reflection of Christ's character and our message will then be characterized by the demonstration of the Spirit's power. It is by becoming one with the Father that we can know peace in the midst of storms. It is through the Lord's abiding presence that we find the secret place of the most high and abide under the shadow of the Almighty. We should earnestly contend for the apostolic principles found in the early church and demonstrated in the life of John G. Lake. This generation has the opportunity to experience the return of our faith to the apostolic pattern. As we consider the days of old and the generations of long ago, we can see firsthand the application of true apostolic ministry available in the days to come.

GREAT HEALING REVIVAL

God has done much in my life and ministry. Healing has been a major part of Revival. God has spoken for years of great healing Revivals breaking out all over the world. In this Chapter I will share about how to be in the right position to be a part of this healing revival and how we can tip the scales so that our lives, our cities, regions and nations capture their hour of visitation.

Awesome things have been happening these past few years because of my encounter with God. The Lord has given me a life of miracles, signs, wonders and healings!

1 Samuel 16:12, 13 And he sent, and brought him in. Now he *was* ruddy, *and* withal of a beautiful countenance, and goodly to look to. And the LORD said, Arise, anoint him: for this *is* he. Then Samuel took the horn of oil, and anointed him in the midst of his brethren: and the Spirit of the LORD came upon David from that day forward. So Samuel rose up, and went to Ramah.

Now we know that when God called David it took 13 years for David to step into fullness and become King over all Israel. It was a thirteen year process.

Having said that, quite often when God does things with prophetic people, their testimony becomes a sign to the church of what He is doing. So as we hear about their encounters, it's God speaking to the church. So, right now, based on what the Lord is releasing in my life I am declaring: kingship, kingship, kingship! It's the apostolic! It's the Lion of the tribe of Judah! There is something about the kingly anointing that we are stepping into this year and it brings authority, real power and real dominion. So the Lord was speaking to me about the kingly anointing.

God began to speak about great men and women of God and the healing revival we will see. Immediately in my mind I thought of William Branham and the day the Voice of Healing was born. And then Gordon Lindsay, A.A. Allan, Jack Coe came to mind and the Voice of Healing of the 1940's and 50's.

Acts 5:12 And by the hands of the apostles were many signs and wonders wrought among the people; (and they were all with one accord in Solomon's porch.

There is something very crucial about signs and wonders, the apostolic, and the kingly anointing. I believe God is watching to see if the church will begin to say, "God, there is a need for the apostolic gift to be restored again to the church." We need to see that it was "by the hands of the apostles many signs and wonders were done among the people."

I don't want to emphasize "apostle" too much but rather the "apostolic" because God has been speaking to the church about the apostolic.

I believe that there is something happening in the area of signs and wonders that is connected to the church beginning to recognize its need for the apostolic and to pray for it to come back into the church. That's the face of the lion. Behold the lion. That's the apostolic ministry of Jesus and it represents kingship. It's the lion of the tribe of Judah. So there is something about that kingly anointing. Luke goes on to say in verse 14 that believers were increasingly added, multitudes of both men and women.

Acts 5:14 And believers were the more added to the Lord, multitudes both of men and women.)

There is a connection between the harvest and signs and wonders. And what's the result? Believers were increasingly added to the body of believers. We've seen some signs and wonders. There have been healing ministries and healing waters but we haven't seen the harvest; not in North America. But God revealed that there is a "harvest dimension" coming that is described in verses 15 and 16 of Acts 5.

Acts 5:15, 16 Insomuch that they brought forth the sick into the streets, and laid *them* on beds and couches, that at the least the shadow of Peter passing by might overshadow some of them. There came also a multitude *out* of the cities round about unto Jerusalem, bringing sick folks, and them which were vexed with unclean spirits: and they were healed every one.

The healing progressed to such a level that the sick were brought into the streets on their beds and couches so that Peter's shadow might fall on them. The Lord said, "Bill, we are moving into that place in healing where My shadow is about to show up." There will be such a dimension in the release of healing that His tangible presence will come! It's like the glory clouds of miracles and the power of the Lord being present to heal. It's a whole lot different than the "gift of healing" that we have when we pray for the sick at the altar. Rather, it's this dimension in which even the very shadow passing by held such a manifestation of how much of God was on a man, that even as he passed by the sick, the Spirit of God in him brought healing to the people on beds and couches. Now think about the shadow of Peter. Think of the word shadow in the same context as when the Holy Spirit came upon Mary and overshadowed her. A shift has happened! It's no longer just about the gift of healing that we have as believers! The realm that we will be walking in can be pictured like this: even as we pass the sick and they are there on beds and couches, there is a realm and a radius of the activity of the kingdom of God around us. It's God's kingdom breaking in and people are reporting healings in area hospitals! I believe that the Holy Spirit is coming to cities and regions and will literally overshadow entire city blocks and entire meetings. I'm contending for that! The Lord spoke to me and said, "I am about to release notable, remarkable miracles!"

Speaking of mere men, Oral Roberts had an incredible healing ministry in the 40's, 50's and 60's. Tens of thousands would attend his meetings. There would be a healing line and they just would bring the sick regardless of what condition they were in. They would just come one by one and sometimes he would be praying until three or four in the morning. "What's your name? What's wrong with your body? Do you believe Jesus can heal you?" Then right in front of all the people he would lay hands on them and they would receive healing. Then he would go to the next one and the next one and the next one asking them the same three questions. Then right in front of all the people he would lay hands on them and they would receive healing and he would go to the next one. He would do this for hours. Many people were healed but not every single person. There were over 100 prominent healing ministries in the 40's and 50's. Almost any night in any major city in America you could find a healing meeting like this. And it went on in great strength for about 12 years. But then competition and jealousy crept in so God just shut it all down. As a result, in the midst of that outpouring, God began turning the taps off in heaven. It was one of the greatest healing movements we have ever seen since the days of Jesus. Then all of a sudden it was over. That was it! We still haven't seen the same dimension in our day. Whole crippled tents of chronic illnesses totally healed! We're talking crippled, mangled bodies, one after another after another and all the people would watch the miracles unfold right before their eyes. Limbs would grow out right in front of the people. That's the kind of miracles that were happening.

Then something happened in Oral Roberts' healing ministry. During one of his meetings he was going down the healing line ready to lay hands on a young boy. Suddenly he just broke down and sobbed and sobbed and sobbed. This is what the Lord told him. "You will never lay hands on another sick person in a meeting like this ever again." Jesus said to him: "The healing ministry is over." That was the shift right there. And so Oral Roberts left the healing ministry and eventually built a university. But here is what many people don't know. The Lord told him, "The people have elevated you above Me and you will never lay hands on another sick person in a meeting like this again." Not that he would never pray for the sick again, but not in a meeting or setting like that. I believe that was the day, officially, that the Voice of Healing was over.

In an encounter I realized that these were like the angels assigned to John G. Lake in Spokane, and to Alexander Dowie in Zion, Illinois and to William Branham in the Voice of Healing. And I realized that these were angels like the angels in John 5 and they were about to be sent to cities, churches, regions and ministries and it was all about the coming healing revival.

John 5:1-4 After this there was a feast of the Jews; and Jesus went up to Jerusalem. Now there is at Jerusalem by the sheep *market* a pool, which is called in the Hebrew tongue Bethesda, having five porches. In these lay a great multitude of impotent folk, of blind, halt, withered, waiting for the moving of the water. For an angel went down at a certain season into the pool, and troubled the water: whosoever then first after the troubling of the water stepped in was made whole of whatsoever disease he had.

In Jerusalem there was a certain place by the sheep gate where there was a pool of water. Multitudes of sick people would go there because an angel would come at certain seasons and stir the water and whoever was the first to step into the water after it was stirred they would be healed. There was something happening in that place. Because the angel, the shadow and the glory cloud came, it was a healing pool, a resident healing pool. An angel came and there was a pool of healing that opened in that place. It could be open in your church, your city, your region and your nation! The angel can come down and be a sign to your life just as it was a sign to Alexander Dowie, John G. Lake and William Branham!

When the waters begin to move in the church in America, great multitudes who are lame and blind and who are waiting for a demonstration of God's power are going to be healed! The kingdom of God is not mere talk but power! We owe the world a demonstration of the Holy Spirit and power! We owe them more than words! There are great multitudes that are waiting for something more than just talk. They are waiting for tangible evidence that there is healing in the church again and then they will come. Remember they came from all over Israel because they said to each other, "There is a place in Jerusalem. There is a pool in the city; one place, a geographical place. We can be healed if we go to that place!"

These angels, I saw them in heaven, and God said, "They are about to be released again. I am going to open up these healing pools." I felt in my spirit that it's not just one, not just two, but why not many healing centers all at the same time in which great multitudes of people would say, "If I could just get to that place in your city. There will be pools in certain places where the angels will come, the healing angels. I believe that God is about to release these pools and whoever steps into the pool will be healed because of the anointing that is in the place.

So I saw these healing angels and the Lord spoke to me and He said, "Bill, I am going to release a healing ministry. I am going to give it to you. I am going to raise you up as a first fruit to pioneer again. You are going to be a sign to the church that there is coming a great healing revival. And everything that you live for is impartation and every place that you go I want you to lay hands on people and I want them to receive this anointing. It's not just a grace that I have placed on your life. It's for the believers, the church, the cities, the regions and the nations. I want you to prophesy about this revival that is coming." I spoke about this in 2009 in a revival in Litchfield, concerning this, the Lord told me, "It has not yet been determined in heaven which cities will receive an outpouring." Jesus wept over Jerusalem because they did not know their hour of visitation.

Luke 19:44 And shall lay thee even with the ground, and thy children within thee; and they shall not leave in thee one stone upon another; because thou knewest not the time of thy visitation.

Jesus was just as willing to come into that city as He was to come into any other city. He had a great healing revival in Capernaum. Every sickness and every disease was healed.

Luke 4:40 Now when the sun was setting, all they that had any sick with divers diseases brought them unto him; and he laid his hands on every one of them, and healed them.

Every sickness and every disease was healed in Capernaum in the region of Naphtali and Zebulun, which was the international head quarters, the missions base for the ministry of Jesus. There was such an anointing in that place by the Sea of Galilee that when the sick came all of them received healing.

Matthew 4:13-17 And leaving Nazareth, he came and dwelt in Capernaum, which is upon the sea coast, in the borders of Zabulon and Nephthalim: That it might be fulfilled which was spoken by Esaias the prophet, saying, The land of Zabulon, and the land of Nephthalim, *by* the way of the sea, beyond Jordan, Galilee of the Gentiles; The people which sat in darkness saw great light; and to them which sat in the region and shadow of death light is sprung up. From that time Jesus began to preach, and to say, Repent: for the kingdom of heaven is at hand.

However, the Bible says that when Jesus went to Nazareth He could do no mighty signs there because of their unbelief.

Matthew 13:58 And he did not many mighty works there because of their unbelief.

What does that tell you? God was just as willing in Nazareth to bring them the same revival. A lot of people say, "It's sovereign. Look at Toronto, Pensacola and the Welsh Revival." The Lord said, "No it wasn't." He said, "It is being determined in heaven right now." God is looking at Cities and nations, whether they are going to be "sheep" cities and nations or "goat" cities and nations are being determined in heaven right now.

Matthew 25:32, 33 And before him shall be gathered all nations: and he shall separate them one from another, as a shepherd divideth *his* sheep from the goats: And he shall set the sheep on his right hand, but the goats on the left.

There is a literal scale in heaven right now and the choices are being determined in heaven even today. We can literally tip the scale for our city! I want to discuss how we can tip the scale and then capture our hour of visitation. I'll pin point several areas that will help us discern what God is actually doing right in this very hour. It's exciting! So keep pressing in and prepare your heart because God wants to reveal to us the great and mighty deeds that He is accomplishing NOW! We don't want to miss one good thing that the Lord is doing!

Hebrews 11:10 For he looked for a city which hath foundations, whose builder and maker *is* God.

Abraham was looking for the city which has foundations whose architect and builder is God, and I believe God is looking for a city where He can establish His righteous foundations, where His healing virtue can flow like a river! God is looking for cities, not just a church or a building. Jesus said that He must preach the kingdom of God in other cities and not just stay in one city, that He was sent to earth for this purpose. Our problem is that we get too strongly focused on a ministry or a building or a church.

Luke 4:43 And he said unto them, I must preach the kingdom of God to other cities also: for therefore am I sent.

We need to throw out the red carpet for the King of Kings and invite Him into our cities! I want my whole city devoted to Jesus Christ! I want my city so filled with the presence of God that people will be asking, have you been to Litchfield? There is something awesome happening in that city!

It would be much easier to stay in our "city of refuge." It would be much easier to stay in the "ark." But my question is this. "Who will go into the places where deep darkness covers the earth and the people?

Isaiah 60:2 For, behold, the darkness shall cover the earth, and gross darkness the people: but the LORD shall arise upon thee, and his glory shall be seen upon thee.

We can get pretty excited about what God is doing in a ministry and how God is using a man, woman or a church.

But God's purposes will come to us in ways that are so much bigger than just one church and one ministry experiencing a visitation from the Lord.

I believe the Lord is about to come in such a way that when His glory begins to fall, pestilence and fever will be driven away. Habakkuk, the prophet, spoke about God coming in that context:

Habakkuk 3:3-5 God came from Teman, and the Holy One from mount Paran. Selah. His glory covered the heavens, and the earth was full of his praise. And *his* brightness was as the light; he had horns *coming* out of his hand: and there *was* the hiding of his power. Before him went the pestilence, and burning coals went forth at his feet.

God is releasing light called the lightning of God, were flashing from His hand. That's where His power was hidden. I believe that is the kind of healing anointing that God is about to release in the church the lightning of God.

God is looking for a company of believers who will say, here I am Lord, send me! Birth it again Lord a healing revival!

We desperately need evidence and a demonstration and a manifestation of the kingdom and we can give our lives for it! We want to be on the front lines and to be pioneers. We want to run ahead of the chariots of Ahab. Not behind, but running ahead! God is releasing again an anointing of accelerations.

1 Kings 18:46 And the hand of the LORD was on Elijah; and he girded up his loins, and ran before Ahab to the entrance of Jezreel.

The Bible declares that the last great revival before the Second Coming of Jesus will be a healing revival! It's a Bible promise!

Malachi 4:2 But unto you that fear my name shall the Sun of righteousness arise with healing in his wings; and ye shall go forth, and grow up as calves of the stall.

The phrase healing in His wings, describes a shadow. This verse is like a picture of the eagle that comes on the nest and hovers over the whole nest. How many of us want God to come and hover over our city? The anointing that comes in a meeting is a blessing. Don't get me wrong. But that anointing will almost be forgotten in light of the Sun (Son) of Righteousness rising with healing in His wings, spreading His wings like an eagle and coming down upon a whole city!

The coming of the Sun of Righteousness with healing in His wings is linked to when Elijah the prophet comes because Malachi goes on to say in verse 5:

Malachi 4:5 Behold, I will send you Elijah the prophet before the coming of the great and dreadful day of the LORD:

What is the coming of the great and dreadful day of the Lord? That's the "second coming" and the spirit of Elijah is going to come before the second coming.

But what's that going to look like, when Elijah comes?

Luke 1:17 And he shall go before him in the **spirit and power of Elias**, to turn the hearts of the fathers to the children, and the disobedient to the wisdom of the just; to make ready a people prepared for the Lord.

Look at what the angel said to Zacharias (about the coming of his son, John the Baptist): "He will also go before Him in the spirit and power of Elijah, to turn the hearts of the fathers to the children, and the disobedient to the wisdom of the just, to make ready a people prepared for the Lord". It's going to look like this: it's the spirit and power of Elijah that will come! This empowerment will come like it came upon John the Baptist.

Matthew 11:12-14 And from the days of John the Baptist until now the kingdom of heaven suffereth violence, and the violent take it by force. For all the prophets and the law prophesied until John. And if ye will receive *it*, this is Elias, which was for to come.

You know why the people almost missed Elijah in this context. Because they were looking for a physical Elijah! And we could miss Elijah's coming again just like they missed it.

Matthew 11:14 And if ye will receive *it*, this is Elias, which was for to come.

Elijah had come already and it was like they said, "What? Where is he John the Baptist? That was Elijah?" Yes! John came in the spirit and power of Elijah.

Luke 1:17 And he shall go before him in the spirit and power of Elias, to turn the hearts of the fathers to the children, and the disobedient to the wisdom of the just; to make ready a people prepared for the Lord.

Elijah will come again in a similar way like when John the Baptist came in the spirit and power of Elijah. As I said earlier, the coming of the Sun of Righteousness with healing in His wings is linked to when Elijah the prophet comes and it will be before the great and dreadful day of the Lord.

I believe that the same anointing and spirit Elijah had will be released once again and it will be in the church. This will be one of the signs of the times that the end is near, that Christ is coming. Yes! We will see that spirit once again and it will be in the church. That same grace to see the same kind of miracles that Elijah saw we'll see in the church, again.

Elijah called down the fire of God in one of the most powerful demonstrations of God's power ever described in the Bible.

1 Kings 18:37-39 Hear me, O LORD, hear me, that this people may know that thou *art* the LORD God, and *that* thou

hast turned their heart back again. Then the fire of the LORD fell, and consumed the burnt sacrifice, and the wood, and the stones, and the dust, and licked up the water that *was* in the trench. And when all the people saw *it,* they fell on their faces: and they said, The LORD, he *is* the God; the LORD, he *is* the God.

God wants to demonstrate His power today. It's a signs and wonders revival that's coming! And before we discuss how this revival is being determined, I want to share a word that the Lord gave me recently. There would be a resident anointing for healing in America with healing pools.

Now I'll examine how this revival is being determined.

Revelations 11:1 And there was given me a reed like unto a rod: and the angel stood, saying, Rise, and measure the temple of God, and the altar, and them that worship therein.

The temple of God is being measured and I believe that the temple of God is us, the church. It's not the physical building. The suggestion here is that John, the apostle, is being told to measure the temple of God, the altar and those who worship there. It's like he is measuring and checking the levels of worship, prayer and intercession. In like manner, today, we need to check the temperature in the churches and in the cities until its just right.

How about your city? What's the temperature? How "hot" is it in your church and your city? There's something about those who worship and pray. Also, there's something about those cities that are having their climate and atmosphere changed because of worship and prayer. In some places there is constant, sustained prayer for 24 hours a day, seven days a week. It's literally breaking open heaven.

I believe there is something that God is releasing today through our worship prayer and intercession. To explain more fully, when the bowls in heaven are filling up with the prayers of the saints, the level of prayer in those bowls will be a sign to the Lord as to where He can assign and release healing pools. So, the level of our prayer and worship is a major determining factor.

Revelations 5:8 And when he had taken the book, the four beasts and four *and* twenty elders fell down before the Lamb, having every one of them harps, and golden vials full of odours, which are the prayers of saints.

Also, God is going to release power, but the measure of power that He releases is determined by the measure of worship and prayer in our lives. So if we want this Elijah anointing, then God is going to measure the levels of worship and intercession in our lives because here is what happens in,

Revelations 11:3 And I will give *power* unto my two witnesses, and they shall prophesy a thousand two hundred *and* threescore days, clothed in sackcloth.

You see, the power that is being released to prophesy is being determined by the worship and prayer. And verse 4 says that the power to prophesy is going to come to the two olive trees and the two lamp stands (which represent the two witnesses).

Revelations 11:4 These are the two olive trees, and the two candlesticks standing before the God of the earth.

Well, who are the two lamp stands? What are lamp stands in the Bible? It's the church. Jesus is standing in the midst of the seven lamp stands and He says that the seven lamp stands are the seven churches

Revelations 1:12, 13 And I turned to see the voice that spake with me. And being turned, I saw seven golden candlesticks; And in the midst of the seven candlesticks *one* like unto the Son of man, clothed with a garment down to the foot, and girt about the paps with a golden girdle.

Revelations 1:20 The mystery of the seven stars which thou sawest in my right hand, and the seven golden candlesticks. The seven stars are the angels of the seven churches: and the seven candlesticks which thou sawest are the seven churches.

The Bible tells us the answer to the great secret about who the two witnesses are. They are the two lamp stands.

Revelations 11:3, 4 And I will give *power* unto my two witnesses, and they shall prophesy a thousand two hundred *and* threescore days, clothed in sackcloth. These are the two olive trees, and the two candlesticks standing before the God of the earth. The two lamp stands are the church and the church is both the Jewish believers and the gentile believers. Jewish believers are usually called Messianic Jews and I believe that the same spirit that was on Elijah (and Moses) is coming again on the Messianic Jews (as well as the gentiles). (We'll take another look at the spirit that was on Elijah in a moment, as well as the anointing that was on Moses.)

Did you know that in Israel right now there isn't one major evangelist? There isn't any major evangelist filling stadiums in Israel moving in the kind of power that Elijah and Moses had.

God has to raise up some apostles, evangelists, prophets, pastors and teachers. I believe that some of the greatest ministries that we are going to see in the end, some of the greatest healing ministries, are going to come out of Israel. And at the same time God is moving on the Gentiles and the believers.

Ephesians 2:11-22 Wherefore remember, that ye *being* in time past Gentiles in the flesh, who are called Uncircumcision by that which is called the Circumcision in the flesh made by hands; That at that time ye were without Christ, being aliens from the commonwealth of Israel, and strangers from the covenants of promise, having no hope, and without God in the world: But now in Christ Jesus ye who sometimes were far off are made nigh by the blood of Christ. For he is our peace, who hath made both one, and hath broken down the middle wall of partition *between us;* Having abolished in his flesh the enmity, *even* the law of commandments *contained* in ordinances; for to make in himself of twain one new man, *so* making peace; And that he might reconcile both unto God in one body by the cross, having slain the enmity thereby: And came and preached peace to you which were afar off, and to them that were nigh. For through him we both have access by one Spirit unto the Father. Now therefore ye are no more strangers and foreigners, but fellowcitizens with the saints, and of the household of God; And are built upon the foundation of the apostles and prophets, Jesus Christ himself being the chief corner *stone;* In whom all the building fitly framed together groweth unto an holy temple in the Lord: In whom ye also are builded together for an habitation of God through the Spirit.

The kind of power that God is going to trust us (the church) with is described in,

Revelations 11:5, 6 And if any man will hurt them, fire proceedeth out of their mouth, and devoureth their enemies: and if any man will hurt them, he must in this manner be killed. These have power to shut heaven, that it rain not in the days of their prophecy: and have power over waters to turn them to blood, and to smite the earth with all plagues, as often as they will.

"And if anyone wants to harm them" means if anyone wants to harm the two witnesses. The two witnesses are the two lamp stands, the church Jewish and Gentile believers who will walk in an incredible power anointing as described in these (immediate) verses. Now, I want to ask three questions relating to these verses. Which two great men of God walked in this same anointing? Who, through the power of God called down fire and stopped the rain from falling? Who through the power of God turned the water into blood and struck the earth with plagues? Elijah and Moses! (1 Kings 17:1, 18:37-39, Exodus 7:20, 8-12.)

It's not just about physical healing; this is about signs and wonders! Can you imagine such a place of partnership with God that as often as we desire, we can be trusted with the kind of anointing that moves heaven and earth and that literally commands weather patterns and rebukes famines. And Moses was a prophet of government leaders and kings. This is an incredible dimension. The same kind of power that God placed upon Moses and Elijah is going to come upon the church again. I believe that it's close.

But many people will fail to see this incredible dimension opening up because they're going to judge and determine revival based on what is happening in one city or the odd city here and there. For instance, it was easy to mark Toronto, Pensacola and other places like Lakeland. We could see revival there. We could trace it. But what's happening today isn't going to be so much about one place but literally it's going to be happening simultaneously around the world. In fact, I believe it's already happening. Revival is already here but we can't trace it the same way we did before because it's not connected to one city and one building. Rather, it's connected to a group of streams that are coming together right now that are moving in power, signs and wonders simultaneously across the earth. It's a moving revival.

This revival is changing from staying in one place like it did in Toronto (and the people come there), to literally moving through hundreds of ministries simultaneously all through the world. I'm seeing this happen already and I believe that we're already experiencing this but many are going to miss it. This is because our idea of how revival comes is so often connected to a place, to a church, or to a city. But this coming revival is connected to people the body of Christ and the saints and it's already here. In some situations, revival isn't "coming" but rather for some of us, revival is already here! If we would change the way we think (our perspective) then we would perceive in our hearts the new way that God is coming.

As well, I realize that we could have a difficult time tracking what God is doing because we're not used to seeing things globally. However, it's through a global focus that we'll be able to determine what God is doing. We're not going to be able to connect it to a place. There will be places and pools, and I believe this revival is happening simultaneously with many different players from many different backgrounds and streams. But if we're too focused on looking at what's happening in our place and our city we're going to miss the global perspective.

There is a global move that is unprecedented right now in harvest. How many of us are hungry for this? It would be easy for some of us to disengage and step back because for some believers it's over their heads and it feels like too many encounters, visitations, words and too much history. But this is so much more than just our individual healing and our own little need.

God is bringing the supernatural realm right to our door, so to speak! We can break something open in our lives and in our cities because there are angels being released at this set time. I've had encounters with an angel I call Healing that I believe was a part of the Voice of Healing, in the days and ministry of William Branham.

We've seen pools of healing, but nothing like what I believe God is going to release. Today we have an opportunity to come before the Lord. By saying "yes" to what He is moving in right now, we can receive something really precious from Him the reality of the supernatural signs and wonders anointing. I want to encourage you to go for it in your heart! The Lord wants us to contend for this anointing for our lives, our churches, our cities and our nations. Let's tip the scales and pray for our cities, regions and nations. We want to take territory in the spirit so that God can release an increase of anointing to usher in healing pools in our cities and a great healing revival.

THE HEALING MANTLE

I used to see maybe one person truly healed every year in my own ministry and then God released His Healing Mantle and the power of God to heal was present everywhere I went. I believe that since God wants to move in healing we need revelation on this powerful mantle.

I will share from first hand experience about God's desire to release His healing power through dynamic, yet differing, methods. I want to release revelation that will challenge you and also bring you into an increased level of authority when it comes to praying for the sick.

There's no time to waste! It's of the utmost importance that we focus on those specific things that the Lord is emphasizing. So, whether you're out in the market place praying for the sick or you feel like a couch potato spiritually, I want to challenge you today to believe God for the ultimate impossible! Get hungry for God and get focused on what God is underscoring. He wants to touch people's lives through you; there's a big harvest out there and the fields are ripening fast! He wants to make you a channel of His blessing and saving grace!

I want to help your faith and create a hunger in you for all that God wants to accomplish through you, I'm going to talk about healing. When sick or dying, people are healed they experience God's love and the Gospel can more easily penetrate their hearts.

Malachi 4:2 But unto you that fear my name shall the Sun of righteousness arise with healing in his wings; and ye shall go forth, and grow up as calves of the stall.

There is another aspect to "healing in His wings" that I want to talk about today. Think of little eaglets in the nest and the mother eagle broods over them, sits upon the nest, and covers them with her wings. The word here for healing in His wings is the same word for abide under the shadow of the almighty.

Strong's Concordance: 4832, 3671, and 6751.

I see this other aspect prophetically like God casting His shadow over an entire congregation, or an entire city block, or an entire city.

What I mean is that God will come with healing in His wings whereby He will cast His healing shadow over entire cities, over entire regions. God will actually "sit" upon entire cities like an eagle and there will come an anointing corporately on regions. That's the kind of healing anointing that is coming. (I'm not talking about a healing anointing that you and I may possess.)

Another illustration of God's healing shadow is found in Acts 5:15:

Acts 5:15 Insomuch that they brought forth the sick into the streets, and laid *them* on beds and couches, that at the least the shadow of Peter passing by might overshadow some of them.

Emphasis must be placed on the word 'overshadow'. It's the same word describing how the Holy Spirit came upon Mary. (Strong's Concordance 1982)

Luke 1:35 And the angel answered and said unto her, The Holy Ghost shall come upon thee, and the power of the Highest shall overshadow thee: therefore also that holy thing which shall be born of thee shall be called the Son of God.

It wasn't the Apostle Peter's shadow. It was the awesome presence of the Holy Ghost that came upon Peter. In other words, the word shadow implies the over enveloping canopy of the Holy Ghost that overshadows a life and creates a healing radius. (For instance, that within perhaps a six foot radius every sick person is healed.)

So let yourself think of a day in which God's healing anointing will come like the Sun of Righteousness because He is going to rise with healing in His wings and it's going to come upon whole cities and whole regions. It will come! He is going to rise in these end days with a healing revival. Furthermore, in the past if the Holy Spirit could overshadow people through Peter, He can do the same with us as He did with Peter.

Now let's go to the book of Habakkuk and look at a powerful promise the kind of healing anointing that God is actually releasing right now.

Habakkuk 3:4, 5 And *his* brightness was as the light; he had horns *coming* out of his hand: and there *was* the hiding of his power. Before him went the pestilence, and burning coals went forth at his feet.

That's the healing presence of Jesus! At the presence of Jesus, sickness is driven out, and all disease is under His feet. At the presence of Jesus, there's going to be an anointing in which God's power will come into meetings and every sickness will be driven out before the anointing. And you know what kind of power it will be? Rays flashing from His hand; for there His power was hidden. That's the lightning of God.

The power of God to heal, as I just explained, can come upon us sovereignly when we come into contact with the Sun of Righteousness (with healing in His wings), and it can come upon us differently, in a tangible way. Let me explain. The word tangible means: capable of being touched; discernible by the touch; material or substantial. There's something about touching, physically touching an object that's dowsed in the healing anointing that releases God's healing power, because the anointing can reside in physical objects.

Matthew 9:20 And, behold, a woman, which was diseased with an issue of blood twelve years, came behind *him,* and touched the hem of his garment:

Matthew 14:36 And besought him that they might only touch the hem of his garment: and as many as touched were made perfectly whole.

2 Kings 13:21 And it came to pass, as they were burying a man, that, behold, they spied a band *of men;* and they cast the man into the sepulchre of Elisha: and when the man was let down, and touched the bones of Elisha, he revived, and stood up on his feet.

Acts 19:11 And God wrought special miracles by the hands of Paul:

I want you to think about that and about the capacity that we have as mere men and women to receive and manifest the fullness of God. That you could be under such an anointing of God's Spirit that your very clothing could carry the presence of Jesus, and when somebody came in contact with your jacket they were healed! Or if someone came in contact with your bones they were healed!

I have had my bible stolen after meetings a few times for the anointing. I got it back but there is a power that can reside in a garment. Did you know when it comes to operating in the gift of healing there is a spiritual dimension, or realm, that God is opening up that He wants you to discover and learn more about? Most people haven't accessed this uncharted realm yet. Let me explain.

I've known of believers that have had healing gifts for years, such as some great old healing evangelists and guys that have been doing evangelistic meetings quite well for years in a certain way. But the particular realm of the spirit that I'm talking about is just a whole different place. We are going to see this unfold in this coming season.

MAINTAIN REVIVAL

Anyone can have some good meetings that they call revival. Revival to continue with momentum takes a perfect obedience to the moving of the Holy Spirit. God's plan for each one of us does not change. The One who calls us is faithful, and He will do it! I have been in some revivals and led a revival that went over two years. It was an outpouring in my own city. The biggest thing I learned was not just how to get revival to come but also to maintain revival.

1 Thessalonians 5:24 Faithful *is* he that calleth you, who also will do *it*.

Things don't always work out the way we think. God's plans still come to pass.

I have discovered that when God births His plans and purposes in our heart, they do not go poof when we fail, if circumstances are bleak, or as the enemy challenges our call or attacks us on our journey. We may let go of a vision, but God does not. Often we become too discouraged and doubt what we know to be true, and sometimes we pitch figurative tents in our own (or another's) backyard of failure, in our sin, or in hard circumstances. But what we have…man what we have is worth fighting for; it is worth building on, it is worth nurturing.

Your destiny, my destiny, the relationship, the anointing, the souls, the harvest, the gifts, the talents it is worth the fight, it is worth rescue, it is worth repentance, it is worth forgiveness, it is worth cultivating, it is worth hanging with God and moving on and moving with God into the manifestation of His promises, for His Own sake.

2 Timothy 1:12 For the which cause I also suffer these things: nevertheless I am not ashamed: for I know whom I have believed, and am persuaded that he is able to keep that which I have committed unto him against that day.

I love hanging out in the Secret Place of the Most High God! The Most High God is Most High, far above all power and all might, far above all principalities and all dominions, and far above every name given in this age and in every age to come. The very Name of God and His very presence is far above every sin and all oppression, every sickness and all disease, above all lack and all poverty. I am still thankful that He is Most High because all things...all things are under His feet.

This I know by experience. Particularly with recent personal challenges it has been good to remember this place of "I can do all things through Christ who gives me strength," the "more than a conqueror" place of victory. It is a place of overcoming, rising up, far above, not defeated; a place of subjecting those things that bind and trip me up to the rule of the Lordship of King Jesus.

The Secret Place...this is where I can completely trust His ability and love, and lay down my own ability and failures at His feet. It is in this High Place of rescue and restoration that I have revisited His plans and purposes for my life, and, where He has resurrected the hope of my calling.

The restorative of God's precious presence is priceless. I am seeing and loving the results as I grow and increase in mature stature in Christ Jesus with firm resolve to lay down my will completely for His. In addition, I have a greater sensitivity to His will, to the need for accountability, and to the needs and feelings of others. Most of all, I am even more determined to glorify His name and lift it ever higher as His subject and as a walking testimony of His continual transforming grace.

I am well aware that the journey from our past mistakes can be burdened with fear, doubt, trepidation, condemnation, and regret, for starters. However, in this divine river, this "Secret Place of His Presence," I have lingered with the Word Face-to-face, and receive power moment-by-moment to live a acceptable life today thus gaining the courage to flow with God and within His will into the places of tomorrow. Pressures, temptations, oppressive forces, sin, and sickness abound but we all have the privilege of resting in the Secret Place of His presence where we can completely trust God's ability and love for us, and lay our ability, will, failures, circumstances, and battles completely at His feet.

I will never know joy unless I am on this journey within His will, in the outflow and overflow of His love, glorifying Him at every juncture, lifting High His banner into the harvest fields. I have learned a lot, and I am growing in the knowledge of His grace. God is restoring His people, and I among them, hallelujah, I believe to prepare us for the greater to come. How I hunger for more of Him and the more of Him the more His love manifests in signs, wonders, and miracles. More than ever now, I see people hungry for the miraculous; but what they are saying is, "I want/need/have to have more of You, Jesus!" Many believers are operating in a greater anointing for deliverance and healing than we have seen in decades, and with significant breakthrough, as we have seen, is only the beginning.

We all desperately need God's touch in every aspect of our lives. I hear how discouragement can foster unbelief. I pray unbelief is not in your heart as a result of hurt and disappointment shaped by unfolding events. You are breaking through, I am breaking through, the Church is breaking through, heaven is breaking through, hell is not prevailing, and things are about to change big time.

I have never felt as free in God as I do right now. Discouragement, especially in these difficult times can be a major hindrance to this restoration of Jesus' deliverance and healing ministry within the Church. Sadly, multitudes in the Body of Christ today suffer all kinds of bondages and sicknesses because of the unbelief in God's power for today, and remain in Egypt. Nevertheless, it is time for all of us to enter the Promised Land, a kingdom demonstrated not just in word but also in power.

If we are to set America ablaze, we need the cutting edge power of God to capture its attention; we need to preach the Gospel of power with signs, wonders, and miracles following.

In a world so immersed in secular humanism and influenced by the media and entertainment industry, we need the power and love of God radically demonstrated in our lives and in our works. I have made it my life's work to know Jesus and the reality of the supernatural power of God on earth as it is in heaven so that my life would become a supernaturally empowered and charged walking, living, breathing testimony that introduces the world to the Supernatural God of Love and Power, the Creator of the Universe who restores people, who desires people whole, delivered and healed. Jesus came to set captives free from their past to their purpose. The more we have to testify of and the more people testifying, the more the world will realize how deep and wide His love, that miracles happen, and prayer works.

I am committed to the work of the Holy Spirit in my life and in yours, to the original vision, to fresh vision, and to His plans and purposes, and look forward to moving with God into His call and going forth in an overflow of miracles with you, for His Name's sake.

SIGNS AND WONDERS OF TODAY

We have seen God's awesome signs and wonders but it is nothing compared to what God is about to release. The Scripture promises, if we draw near to Him.He will draw near to us. That is the "one thing" that characterized King David's life and the hungry heart he possessed. David loved the Lord's presence more than anything else; for that the Lord loved and trusted him. Devotion to be identified as God's "friend" is our most noble pilgrimage.

John 15:15 Henceforth I call you not servants; for the servant knoweth not what his lord doeth: but I have called you friends; for all things that I have heard of my Father I have made known unto you.

Even so, we are also given clear and concise biblical affirmations of the functioning of His victorious Church. There is a mandate placed upon the latter-day Church to gather the harvest and awaken a misguided generation to its righteous destiny. To accomplish this, we must be endowed with Heaven's virtue and empowered with the overcoming victory of the Lord's redemptive work. There is a clear revelation of Jesus Christ and His word that is validated with biblical confirmations. The Lord's example and demonstration of mighty works are necessary for this inevitable responsibility and as He promised, even greater works.

John 14:12 Verily, verily, I say unto you, He that believeth on me, the works that I do shall he do also; and greater *works* than these shall he do; because I go unto my Father.

The gospel of the Kingdom is the power of God leading to salvation. This gospel does not merely consist in words but also in God's sovereign power. The ministry of signs and wonders does not diminish the supernatural of God's written word; it only confirms it. God's revealed word is plainly established by the Holy Spirit's endorsement. He demonstrates approval or affirmation through signs, wonders and manifestations of the Spirit. According to the writer of Hebrews, the Lord's Spirit works with His people by, testifying with them, both by signs and wonders and by various miracles and by gifts of the Holy Spirit according to His own will.

Hebrews 2:4 God also bearing *them* witness, both with signs and wonders, and with divers miracles, and gifts of the Holy Ghost, according to his own will?

God's power and witness is fundamentally necessary for us to accomplish Heaven's blueprint. We simply do not posses the ability within ourselves to accomplish God's ultimate plan. We need God and the personification of His Spirit that provides power. Even so, as wonderful and necessary as incredible displays of the Spirit are, we can not allow that to supersede our quest to know Him as the Living Word.

John G. Lake was a man used powerfully as a missionary to South Africa and healing evangelist throughout America. History now documents wonderful miracles and spiritual wonders that the Lord achieved through this humble servant. Nevertheless, in 1925 he discerned that his generation "missed the mark" by being more captured by the phenomena of God than the Person. The same was true in the days of Moses when he said, Deuteronomy 29:2-4 And Moses called unto all Israel, and said unto them, Ye have seen all that the LORD did before your eyes in the land of Egypt unto Pharaoh, and unto all his servants, and unto all his land; The great temptations which thine eyes have seen, the signs, and those great miracles: Yet the LORD hath not given you an heart to perceive, and eyes to see, and ears to hear, unto this day.

Consequently, there must be a balance in our personal endeavor to know the Lord and our mandate to win this generation through the Spirit's demonstration of power. Through fellowship with Him our spiritual senses become keenly sensitive to His voice and the message being confirmed through signs and wonders. These birthrights must be maintained in the proper biblical order.

The ministry of the early church was profound on many levels. By natural standards, the credentials of the individuals utilized were not impressive. For the most part, their personal abilities left them unqualified for their pioneering assignment. Even so, they received an impartation from God that validated their mission and facilitated the revelation of God's Kingdom.

They believed God and trusted not in their own strength, but in His.

The Bible plainly outlines the many signs and miraculous wonders that accompanied the early Church in their task. The Scripture tells us that reverential awe fell upon many as miraculous wonders took place. People were added to the Church daily and God's name was notably glorified. These are the same results we need today. Our task is no less important or difficult than the one given to the early Apostolic Church. In fact, in many ways ours is even more intense. Therefore, we need all that the early church had and in multiplied fashion. The early disciples preached the Gospel of the Kingdom and ministered to people's spirit, soul and body. They did not "shrink from declaring the whole purpose of God." In the midst of persecution and an unbelieving generation, their message was confirmed with the Holy Spirit's power imparted to them on the Day of Pentecost. It was their prayer that the Lord would, grant to Your servants that with all boldness they may speak Your word, by stretching out Your hand to heal, and that signs and wonders may be done through the name of Your holy Servant Jesus.

Acts 4:29, 30 And now, Lord, behold their threatenings: and grant unto thy servants, that with all boldness they may speak thy word, By stretching forth thine hand to heal; and that signs and wonders may be done by the name of thy holy child Jesus.

God's power is a witness to the gospel. That is why the early Church passionately prayed to be empowered with signs and wonders as an instrument to convey the good news of the Kingdom and win the lost. In each expression of spiritual outpouring throughout church history, God's Presence was authenticated with various expressions of His Spirit. During the early 20th century, Maria Woodworth Etter's ministry was characterized by wonderful manifestations of spiritual signs and miraculous wonders like the early apostolic believers. Marvelous displays of healing and deliverance were prevalent in her meetings. Additionally, it was not uncommon for many people to "fall under the power" and remain in that condition for many days. The Bible promised to "bear witness" to the Kingdom message with divers and various miracles and gifts of the Holy Spirit.

Hebrews 2:4 God also bearing *them* witness, both with signs and wonders, and with divers miracles, and gifts of the Holy Ghost, according to his own will?

Oftentimes doctors would examine the people while in this condition to determine their heart rate and other vital statistics. In each case it was reported that every individual was in a perfectly healthy state. They were overshadowed with God's Spirit and face down before God without food, water or movement. It was reported that in some cases people remained in this condition for as long as seven days. This was confirmed by both the secular and Christian media. Tremendous testimonies of healing, deliverance and divine commissions were reported following the encounters. It was well documented that while experiencing these signs and wonders many people would be commissioned to foreign lands and come out of the experience able to fluently speak the language of the nation to which they were sent. Furthermore, many accounts report the spirit of conviction that accompanied these manifestations to such an extent that the most hardened characters melted into weeping repentance. This was a token of the heritage of God's people and the empowerment of His presence essential in the fulfillment of our latter day mandate. There presently exists an elevated atmosphere of anticipation and encouragement for this generation to experience profound expressions of God's power. We are promised a visitation of God's presence to awaken the Church to her end-time responsibility and influence. We are now beginning to see more evidence of this in the Western Church.

According to Proverbs 29:18, where there is no vision, the people are unrestrained and perish. This Hebrew phrase conveys the necessity for the spirit of revelation to exist in God's people for there to be advancement. The word used for "vision" implies "open vision" communicating God's heart and strategic design. Revelation provides spiritual eyes that see and ears that hear, thereby facilitating hearts with comprehension. Current prophetic messages of hope and destiny provide encouragement to leadership and the Lord's body. The battles have been long and tiresome. The Lord is granting wonderful tokens of confidence to position us for our spiritual release. Naturally, these unusual signs and wonders do not occur needlessly. There must be some fruit or affirmation that is generated advances God's kingdom. The Lord very often allows manifestations of His Spirit with signs and wonders as:

An encouragement to the faith of His people

A witness to the messages presented and their present emphasis

Mobilization of His body into His plan and into their destiny

Spiritual Awakening to the lost and lukewarm

Hebrews 13:1, 2 Let brotherly love continue. Be not forgetful to entertain strangers: for thereby some have entertained angels unawares.

The Bible records countless instances of angelic appearances that marked seasons of transition and advancement. This is especially true in the early Apostolic Church. There is an essential cooperation between Heaven and earth.

We discover in the Gospel of Luke the Lord Jesus walking along the road to Emmaus in "another form." The two disciples did not recognize Him until He came into their home and broke bread before them.

We also notice in the book of Acts the supernatural deliverance of Peter from jail. As he came to the home of the disciples, the young girl who opened the door was startled to see what she perceived was Peter. Upon reporting this to the other disciples they responded that it must have been his angel. This clearly implies that there must have been spiritual messengers working with them who took the form and appearance of the disciples.

This gospel of the Kingdom was first declared by the Lord and evidenced by the Holy Spirit and endorsed by God. He showed His approval of the gospel of power through signs and wonders and miraculous manifestations of the heavenly realm. Angelic appearances and supernatural signs awaken people from apathy and lethargy and reignite hearts that have grown cold or lukewarm to this reality.

It is not our intent to overly emphasize signs and wonders but the messages they convey. There must also be a genuine fruitfulness that comes from the manifestation of the Spirit.

To more fully understand our mission and function on earth, we must also comprehend God's motivation. Our Heavenly Father's desire is to display His glory and bring to His son the full measure of His reward. This is accomplished through the preaching of His word and the testimony of His power. When our motivations are firmly planted in the Lord's heart, then we are biblically justified when we long to see manifestations of His Spirit that glorify His name and convey salvation to the lost. The book of Acts alone records many instances of conversions birthed out of supernatural encounters. Ultimately, our highest purpose in existence is to delight in God and display the essence of who He is to a needy generation. We simply cannot accomplish this mandate in our own strength. We need His empowering Presence and the vindication of His Spirit.

REVIVAL OF THE BOOK OF ACTS

We are supposed to be like the Early Church turning the world upside down. Since we are supposed to continue the writings of the book of Acts, let's take a look at the great revival that took place. This is mainly a Chapter of scripture but read it and you will be encouraged to press in for more of God.

Mark 3:14, 15 And he ordained twelve, that they should be with him, and that he might send them forth to preach, And to have power to heal sicknesses, and to cast out devils:
 1st. To preach the Gospel.
 2nd. To be the physician of souls.
 3rd. To wage war with the devil, and destroy his kingdom.
 Mark 16:17-20 And these signs shall follow them that believe; In my name shall they cast out devils; they shall speak with new tongues; They shall take up serpents; and if they drink any deadly thing, it shall not hurt them; they shall lay hands on the sick, and they shall recover. So then after the Lord had spoken unto them, he was received up into heaven, and sat on the right hand of God. And they went forth, and preached every where, the Lord working with them, and confirming the word with signs following. Amen.

Acts 1:8 But ye shall receive power, after that the Holy Ghost is come upon you: and ye shall be witnesses unto me both in Jerusalem, and in all Judaea, and in Samaria, and unto the uttermost part of the earth.

Acts 2:1-5 And when the day of Pentecost was fully come, they were all with one accord in one place. And suddenly there came a sound from heaven as of a rushing mighty wind, and it filled all the house where they were sitting. And there appeared unto them cloven tongues like as of fire, and it sat upon each of them. And they were all filled with the Holy Ghost, and began to speak with other tongues, as the Spirit gave them utterance. And there were dwelling at Jerusalem Jews, devout men, out of every nation under heaven.

Acts 2:17, 18 And it shall come to pass in the last days, saith God, I will pour out of my Spirit upon all flesh: and your sons and your daughters shall prophesy, and your young men shall see visions, and your old men shall dream dreams: And on my servants and on my handmaidens I will pour out in those days of my Spirit; and they shall prophesy:

Acts 2:43-47 And fear came upon every soul: and many wonders and signs were done by the apostles. And all that believed were together, and had all things common; And sold their possessions and goods, and parted them to all men, as every man had need. And they, continuing daily with one accord in the temple, and breaking bread from house to house, did eat their meat with gladness and singleness of heart, Praising God, and having favour with all the people. And the Lord added to the church daily such as should be saved.

Acts 3:1-10 Now Peter and John went up together into the temple at the hour of prayer, being the ninth hour. And a certain man lame from his mother's womb was carried, whom they laid daily at the gate of the temple which is called Beautiful, to ask alms of them that entered into the temple; Who seeing Peter and John about to go into the temple asked an alms. And Peter, fastening his eyes upon him with John, said, Look on us. And he gave heed unto them, expecting to receive something of them. Then Peter said, Silver and gold have I none; but such as I have give I thee: In the name of Jesus Christ of Nazareth rise up and walk. And he took him by the right hand, and lifted him up: and immediately his feet and ankle bones received strength. And he leaping up stood, and walked, and entered with them into the temple, walking, and leaping, and praising God. And all the people saw him walking and praising God: And they knew that it was he which sat for alms at the Beautiful gate of the temple: and they were filled with wonder and amazement at that which had happened unto him.

Acts 3:19-21 Repent ye therefore, and be converted, that your sins may be blotted out, when the times of refreshing shall come from the presence of the Lord; And he shall send Jesus Christ, which before was preached unto you: Whom the heaven must receive until the times of restitution of all things, which God hath spoken by the mouth of all his holy prophets since the world began.

Acts 4:13, 14 Now when they saw the boldness of Peter and John, and perceived that they were unlearned and ignorant men, they marvelled; and they took knowledge of them, that they had been with Jesus. And beholding the man which was healed standing with them, they could say nothing against it.

Acts 4:31, 32 And when they had prayed, the place was shaken where they were assembled together; and they were all filled with the Holy Ghost, and they spake the word of God with boldness. And the multitude of them that believed were of one heart and of one soul: neither said any of them that ought of the things which he possessed was his own; but they had all things common.

Acts 5:12-20 And by the hands of the apostles were many signs and wonders wrought among the people; (and they were all with one accord in Solomon's porch. And of the rest durst no man join himself to them: but the people magnified them. And believers were the more added to the Lord, multitudes both of men and women.) Insomuch that they brought forth the sick into the streets, and laid them on beds and couches, that at the least the shadow of Peter passing by might overshadow some of them. There came also a multitude out of the cities round about unto Jerusalem, bringing sick folks, and them which were vexed with unclean spirits: and they were healed every one. Then the high priest rose up, and all they that were with him, (which is the sect of the Sadducees,) and were filled with indignation, And laid their hands on the apostles, and put them in the common prison. But the angel of the Lord by night opened the prison doors, and brought them forth, and said, Go, stand and speak in the temple to the people all the words of this life.

Acts 5:40-42 And to him they agreed: and when they had called the apostles, and beaten them, they commanded that they should not speak in the name of Jesus, and let them go. And they departed from the presence of the council, rejoicing that they were counted worthy to suffer shame for his name. And daily in the temple, and in every house, they ceased not to teach and preach Jesus Christ.

Acts 8:4-8 Therefore they that were scattered abroad went every where preaching the word. Then Philip went down to the city of Samaria, and preached Christ unto them. And the people with one accord gave heed unto those things which Philip spake, hearing and seeing the miracles which he did. For unclean spirits, crying with loud voice, came out of many that were possessed with them: and many taken with palsies, and that were lame, were healed. And there was great joy in that city.

Acts 19:6-12 And when Paul had laid his hands upon them, the Holy Ghost came on them; and they spake with tongues, and prophesied. And all the men were about twelve. And he went into the synagogue, and spake boldly for the space of three months, disputing and persuading the things concerning the kingdom of God. And God wrought special miracles by the hands of Paul: So that from his body were brought unto the sick handkerchiefs or aprons, and the diseases departed from them, and the evil spirits went out of them.

WILLIAM BRANHAM

God had me spend the most part of a year studying all I could on the man William Branham. We can learn for great men and women of old. I cannot talk about the healing revival without looking at the man and ministry of William Branham. During the early 1930s an extraordinarily gifted prophet began to emerge as a spiritual leader of a new ministry model. His name was William Branham. He was a man raised in Kentucky and ordained as a Baptist minister. Even so, God wonderfully graced this humble man with a revelatory gift and supernatural power not seen since the early Church.

Not only were the miracles and healings that accompanied his ministry astounding, but he was also shown numerous future events with remarkable accuracy that now are a matter of historical record.

Following a series of evangelistic meetings, Branham held a baptismal service on June 11, 1933, for new converts. Some four thousand people lined the banks of the Ohio River to observe and celebrate the service. While baptizing the seventeenth person, whirling amber light descended from Heaven and rested directly above Branham. Virtually all the witnesses present could see this supernatural sign. Many eyewitnesses ran in fear, while others fell to their knees and worshipped because they recognized this was God doing something truly extraordinary. In this experience God gave William Branham a forerunner message for his life and ministry. I believe he was a token or prototype of an entire body of people who will emerge as Jesus' bridal company.

By his own acknowledgment, Branham was a forerunner of something new and fresh the Lord planned for the last days. This supernatural dimension will be commonplace in end-time life and ministry.

Numerous news organizations picked up the story and circulated it around the U.S. and Canada. One headline read, "Mysterious Light Appears over Baptist Minister While Baptizing in the Ohio River." The Evening News reported the incident with the subheading, "Mysterious Star Appears over Minister While Baptizing." Though many may debate the full meaning of the event, its authenticity is not disputed.

This public display of God's awesome power framed a heavenly intention. No design of Heaven is ever administered uselessly. Every word and demonstration that proceeds from the mouth and hand of God will return fruitfully. A Kingdom message for today's Church was sent to that prior generation and we are responsible for it coming forth. The Living Word desires to rest in His bride. Jesus wants to become flesh once more and demonstrate His Kingdom power and redemptive virtue.

If that episode on the Ohio River was just an isolated incident then we could be thrilled by such a display of God's power and move on. However, that was only one of many expressions of God in the life of this forerunner.

During his early ministry, Branham had several supernatural experiences for which he had no way to reference or ability to understand. Neither he nor those with who he was in ministry relationship comprehended the revelatory realm of God. Only the Bible provided any source of enlightenment; very few people had personally experienced this supernatural dimension of God. Unfortunately, most Christians at the time believed those kinds of expressions had happened in the Bible but did not any longer. Words like trance and vision rarely existed in the spiritual language of that day. During this time few people had access to libraries or Christian material. Branham was very in the early years and certainly had no way of researching how God's supernatural power had manifested throughout Church history. Nonetheless, the Spirit showed him things that would occur in the future. He shared those encounters openly with those around him. To everyone's amazement, the events came to pass in precisely the manner he predicted. Tremendous healings frequently accompanied his revelatory experiences.

It wasn't until an angelic visitation, that Branham came to understand more fully the purpose and validity of the supernatural dimension into which he had been thrust. This minister of God was desperate to understand the spiritual realms he was witnessing or he would die trying. He set his intent on discovering whether his visions and trances were from God or from the enemy. He loved the Lord too much to allow deception to rule him.

Branham withdrew to a secluded wooded area in rural Indiana. There was no food, electricity, or other provision.

All he did was lay before God in humility and sincerity. Wonderfully, the Lord answered the cry of His servant.

An angel was sent to Branham and told him about his life and calling in a face to face encounter. This heavenly messenger came to impart spiritual understanding and a divine commission.

According to Branham's personal testimony which he often shared publicly during the late '40s and throughout the '50s, something supernatural occurred late that night after many hours of prayer. A heavenly light appeared; it looked like an amber or emerald star of fire, illuminating the room around him. It was the same manifestation that had appeared over the Ohio River thirteen years earlier. At that moment Branham heard footsteps walking toward him and saw someone standing in the light. An angelic messenger greeted him as in the Bible: "Fear not, for I am sent from the presence of Almighty God." The angel, according to Branham, was six feet tall and weighed approximately two hundred pounds. He had an olive complexion, with dark hair that touched his shoulders, and he wore a white robe that reached to his feet. As soon as Branham heard the greeting, he recognized the angel's voice as the one he had heard throughout his youth and early ministry.

The Lord was looking for a messenger to fulfill a divine mandate and to introduce the supernatural dimension of Heaven to a new generation. Clearly the humility and devotion of Branham captured Heaven's attention and opened the door for this man to be used in significant ways. A plan, initiated before the foundation of the world, was set in motion for him. The time had arrived for destiny to be fulfilled.

The angel informed Branham that he was called to take a message of divine healing around the world. The angel promised him that if he could get people to believe, nothing would hinder the fulfillment of his prayers-not even cancer. Branham introduced his generation, and ours, to the revelatory realm of Heaven. These signs and wonders acted as a platform to birth faith in the supernatural power of God.

Notable supernatural impartation was released during this visitation. The angel told him that just like Moses, he would be given two gifts as signs of this impartation. Whenever he took a person's right hand with his left, he would by revelation perceive the person's physical condition. This was the first spiritual gift: it allowed the minister to detect through revelatory insight the specific illnesses, demonic oppressions, and deadly diseases afflicting the people.

Whenever Branham prophesied a illness or condition, his listeners' faith in God was elevated, allowing incredible healing and miracles. His first public healing meeting after his commissioning took place in St. Louis, Missouri. Immediately creative miracles and demonstrations of healing, were generated on such a massive scale that theologians termed it an unprecedented event in Church history. As Gordon Lindsay once said, "there were no hard cases." No matter how severe the difficulty, the Lord was present to heal.

The angel promised Branham that God would give him a second gift if he used the first with humility. The next gift gave him discernment of thoughts and secrets of the heart and would take people to an even deeper level of faith.

As Jesus' encounter with the Samaritan woman at the well had, the unfolding of personal history and intimate secrets ignited faith. People rose above shame and unbelief and engaged the revelatory realm of Heaven. Their response is a prophetic model for our generation.

The Bible declares that the living Word is alive, active, and a discerner of the thoughts and desires of the heart.

Hebrews 4:12 For the word of God *is* quick, and powerful, and sharper than any twoedged sword, piercing even to the dividing asunder of soul and spirit, and of the joints and marrow, and *is* a discerner of the thoughts and intents of the heart.

The gift of discernment offers a far greater dimension in God than the expression of a simple "word of knowledge." It is a reflection that the Lord has removed the veil dividing soul and spirit, and all things are open and exposed to Him.

When operating in the gift of revelatory discernment, Branham would stand before the people and communicate, by supernatural insight, their name, illness, history, address, private prayers and desires, and many other secrets known only to the Lord. Those present in those meetings testify that this dimension of God generated a tangible expectation of faith. People believed that anything was possible in such an atmosphere of heavenly anointing. I've seen videos of

William Branham over and over again. You can still feel God's presence every time.

The messenger from Heaven shared many things with Branham during their lengthy conversation. Branham's ministry introduced a different dimension in God, not seen or demonstrated on such a scale at any time throughout Church history. Its foundation was a union with Christ, with the Lord living in the midst of His people and doing, through them, the same works that He did while on earth.

Gordon Lindsay, founder of Christ for the Nations, wrote of this spiritual experience: "The results of the angelic visitation to William Branham have been a steadily rising tide of revival that has sounded out throughout the world, and the end is not yet."

Following his angelic encounter, Branham emerged with a deep anointing of revelation and power that directly or indirectly touched millions of people and launched a worldwide revival. Countless thousands were miraculously healed of the most hideous infirmities and deadly diseases during the ministry of this man and others who followed.

Naturally God puts His great treasures in earthen vessels. Like all human beings with the exception of Jesus Christ Branham made mistakes and missteps along the way. Even so, his revelatory encounters were marked with mysterious accuracy. It is the revelation of Heaven that is of paramount importance. But just as important is the proper stewardship of the treasures of insight and wisdom with application today; we must carefully unfold God's blueprint.

A divine presence distinguished Branham's life and ministry. The living Word discerned, and communicated through Branham, the thoughts of the heart with profound precision. He was given glimpses into the plan and destiny of Heaven for individuals and corporate bodies. His ministry was a forerunner model that foresaw the impact of a body of believers who will emerge in our day and embody the living Word. The signs and wonders that follow will release a bridal revival that will be identified according to John 14:12 a greater works generation.

It is always wonderful to recount stories of God's goodness to people. However, there is much more for us to understand about God's dealings with Branham's generation. A platform had been established for heavenly truth, and we must comprehend the significance of this type of ministry for our generation. These events were much more than revival; they were the beginning of end time ministry; they pointed to a generation of destiny prophesied in Scripture. As with Moses, these signs were given so that the people would believe. The time has come to revisit the awesome visions given to this godly man, along with the other pieces of the divine puzzle entrusted to other Christians. Like Daniel studying the prophecies of Jeremiah, we should meditate upon these supernatural encounters to extract their application to both Branham's time and our own. We can learn from past mistakes and extract the seeds of God, replanting them in the soil of our honest and sincere hearts.

As in the days of Moses and the Lord Jesus, the enemy recognizes times and seasons that mark the appearance of spiritual deliverers. He wants to snuff out those endowed with the virtue of Heaven to carry out the plan of God.

A day of destiny is upon us. The victorious ones mentioned in the prophecies of Joel are being prepared to emerge as an army, the bridal company joined to the Bridegroom.

THE HEALING MOVEMENT

The Healing Movement that God is releasing will make all the movements look like if they were all combined. The Lord revealed to me a coming Healing revival and spoke to me about a transferable healing anointing. We have seen a tremendous release of healing and an impartation of the anointing for signs and wonders.

I want to share with you several things that the Lord is looking for in restoring the Voice of healing and a healing revival. I believe God is about to release three things the voice, a movement and the creative word!

The voice: The Lord showed me that the eyes of the Lord run to and fro throughout the earth to show himself strong on behalf of the heart contrite before him. God is looking for a John the Baptist, one to show himself strong in power, The voice of one crying out the truth about divine healing without compromise and the fear of the controversy that can come with a ministry of healing. We need preachers of faith, power and the uncompromising gospel! We as a North American church are in a famine of power wilderness God is looking for those who will resurrect the pure word about healing, regardless of what there experience with healing has been, good or bad. We need a restoration of the word faith. I am not talking about the full movement but the heart and spirit behind teachings from men like TJ Osborn and John G Lake. We have a diluted message. We are afraid of the controversy of really believing the lord for healing and preaching the full gospel of miracles, signs and wonders. We are too concerned about those who don't get healed and what about my experience with healing? It is time to open the truth of redemption again and commit our lives to preaching the word of power, even in the midst of little fruit and a label that can come if you really practice "Faith". When I made a decision to believe Jesus for Miracles I decided in my heart that if I prayed for hundreds and no one was healed I would pray for hundreds more, and if all my experience said the message of healing was not for all but some "I would say all" and hold fast to the confession of my faith, though all are not "yet" healed. Who will preach divine healing? There is a huge price with it, victory and defeat. When John the Baptist was beheaded, Jesus continued to heal the sick. When my mother died of a stroke, we have seen many healed of stroke, I refused to have to understand it, I refused discouragement, failure and hopelessness and the question why Lord? All the more I made a commitment to hate disease. My message will never change. I may never have all the absolute answers on why all are not healed but I will fight hurdle through the word of truth movement. In the 1940s-60's there was a incredible release of healing, evangelism and power. Hundreds were raised up and began to blaze across America with signs and wonders, including Jack Coe, Oral Roberts, William Branham and Gordon Lindsay and many more. This was a healing revival and I believe few if any are walking in the anointing the Holy Spirit released in that time. It was said at one time that more than 100 wheelchairs were emptied in one service and in another service every sickness, crippled body, blind and deaf were healed in one service without the laying on of hands. I believe that God is about to open up that well. The key to mass evangelism is healing, signs and wonders. The Lord showed me two things about this coming movement.

Pools of Bethesda. The name Bethesda means outpouring, I see such an outpouring of the healing anointing that there would be Spokane Washington's across the nations, cities of refuge, whole cities known for healing and the ministry of Jesus. For those who do not know about Spokane in the early 1900s John G Lake started the healing rooms. In 5 years people came from all over the world to be healed and they declared Spokane wash, the healthiest city in America. They documented over 100,000 healings and miracles.

The module of John Lake: Teams of healers and a tangible transferable healing anointing resting even on the children. It is time to train and equip the body of Christ to function as the body of Jesus and Preach the gospel, Heal the sick, Cleanse the Leper and Raise the dead, cast out demons. The John Lake module is a Healing team!

Creative word: There are two things about the creative word. One God is about to release the healing "spoken" word and two he is about to bring us back to the revelation of the healing connected to what we say with our mouth (confession).

It is time that we believe that "he sent his word and delivered them from their destruction's, just say the word and my servant will be healed. Jesus commands us to heal the sick!!! The Lord really challenged me to make open opportunity to command those that are sick and not even physically present in a service to be made whole. The Lord said the more I had people "stand in the gap" and bring aprons and prayer clothes according to Acts 19:11 to our services, the more he would touch the sick that were not present in a service.

We need to prophesy to the sick, speak to the bodies about the change that is coming and how the body will respond to the word of the Lord. We pray to much for God to do what he told us to do, We need to pray until we are full of the Holy Ghost and then go and say cancer leave, deaf hear and blind see in the name of Jesus. It is time to be who God told us we were and stop praying for the sick, oh God do something, and do you want to heal Lord, please heal her Jesus. We need to take more of an authoritative role and command miracles and speak to the dead rise in the name of Jesus!

Proverbs 18:21 Death and life are in the power of the tongue: and they that love it shall eat the fruit thereof. We need life words, Faith words, and God's word.

Proverbs 12:14 A man shall be satisfied with good by the fruit of *his* mouth: and the recompence of a man's hands shall be rendered unto him.

Proverbs 12:18 There is that speaketh like the piercings of a sword: but the tongue of the wise *is* health.

Proverbs 23:7 For as he thinketh in his heart, so *is* he: Eat and drink, saith he to thee; but his heart *is* not with thee.

We need to understand a fresh revelation of the power of our words and what we say is what we are.

Something begins to happen in our heart and spirit when we line ourselves up with what God says and that is what we say. I am what he says I am, and I can do what he says I can. We need to change our mindset and make a decision to renew our minds, hold fast to the confession of our faith in the midst of opposite experience and circumstances. The bible is true!

God is looking for a Voice. A man who will commit their lives to believing for healing, preach the word the truth about divine healing. God is also going to bring a fresh movement to the body of Christ beyond what we have ever experienced in the ministry of Jesus. In this Healing revival God will release the creative word and bring back healing as we have a fresh revelation of the power of what we say.

ABOUT THE AUTHOR

Bill Vincent is an Apostle and Author with Revival Waves of Glory Ministries in Litchfield, IL. Bill and his wife Tabitha work closely in every day ministry duties. Bill and Tabitha lead a team providing Apostolic over sight in all aspects of ministry, including service, personal ministry and Godly character.

Bill is a believer in Jesus Christ in the fullness of power with signs and wonders. Bill has an accurate prophetic gift, a powerful revelatory preaching anointing with miracles signs and wonders following.

Bill Vincent is no stranger to understanding the power of God, having spent over twenty years as a Minister with a strong prophetic anointing, which taught him the importance of deliverance by the power of God. Bill has more than thirty prophetic books available all over the world. Prior to starting his ministry, Revival Waves of Glory he spent the last few years as a Pastor of a Church and a traveling prophetic ministry.

Bill Vincent helps the Body of Christ to get closer to God while overcoming the enemy. Bill offers a wide range of writings and teachings from deliverance, to the presence of God and Apostolic cutting edge Church structure. Drawing on the power of the Holy Spirit through years of experience in Revival, Spiritual Sensitivity and deliverance ministry, Bill now focuses mainly on pursuing the Presence of God and breaking the power of the devil off of people's lives.

His book Defeating the Demonic Realm was published in 2011 and has since helped many people to overcome the spirits and curses of satan. Since then Bill's books have flooded the market with his writings released just like he prophesies the Word of the Lord.

Bill is available for Revival Meetings by going to http://www.revivalwavesofglory.com/Invite-Bill-Vincent.html just fill out the form and email it to billvincent@revivalwavesofglory.com or mail to Revival Waves of Glory PO Box 596 Litchfield, IL 62056. Someone will contact you with any questions or response to request.

Bill Vincent is a unique man of God whom has discovered; powerful ways to pursue God's presence, releasing revelations of the demonic realm and prophetic anointing through everything he does. Bill is always moving forward at a rapid pace and there is sure to be much more released by him in upcoming years.

RECOMMENDED PRODUCTS

By Bill Vincent
Overcoming Obstacles
Glory: Pursuing God's Presence
Defeating the Demonic Realm
Increasing Your Prophetic Gift
Increasing Your Anointing
Keys to Receiving Your Miracle
The Supernatural Realm
Waves of Revival
Increase of Revelation and Restoration
The Resurrection Power of God
Discerning Your Call of God
Apostolic Breakthrough
Glory: Increasing God's Presence
Love is Waiting—Don't Let Love Pass You By
The Healing Power of God
Glory: Expanding God's Presence
Receiving Personal Prophecy
Signs and Wonders
Signs and Wonders Revelations
Children Stories
I Married Jezebel
Rapture Revelations
The Secret Place of God's Power
Building a Prototype Church
Breakthrough of Spiritual Strongholds
Glory: Revival Presence of God
The Watchman of the Lord
Overcoming the Power of Lust

By Bill Vincent—Spanish & French Translation
Love is Waiting—Don't Let Love Pass You By
Signs and Wonders Revelations
I Married Jezebel
Increasing Your Prophetic Gift
Receiving Personal Prophecy

By Bill Vincent, Paula Loveless, Joseph Basurto, Dawn Vitale and Jackie Money
Experience God's Love

By Bishop Gregory Leachman
God's Greatest Challenge:
Man & His Ungodly Ways
Conforming to the Mind of Christ

By Richard Money
My Life in a Salami Factory

Web Site:
www.revivalwavesofgloryministries.com

Mail Order:
Revival Waves of Glory
PO Box 596
Litchfield, IL 62056

Shipping $5.00
Prices do not include shipping and are subject to change. If you mail an order and pay by check, make check out to Revival Waves of Glory.

www.ingramcontent.com/pod-product-compliance
Lightning Source LLC
Chambersburg PA
CBHW070122080526
44586CB00013B/1355